Other Helen Exley Giftbooks

Utterly Lovable Dogs   Glorious Cats
Cat Quotations   Cat Quips
The Littlest Cat Book   To a very special Friend
Dog Quotations   Words on true Happines
Words on the power of Friendship   For a Good Friend
A Little Book of Crafty Cats   Puppies!

Also published by Helen Exley Giftbooks with distinctive
photography by Hanadeka: Utterly Lovable Dogs

By Stuart and Linda Macfarlane

Published simultaneously in 2004 by Exley Publications Ltd in Great Britain,
and Exley Publications LLC in the USA.

Photography copyright © Yoneo Morita 2004 Hanadeka™
Licensed through Intercontinental Licensing
Text © Stuart and Linda Macfarlane 2004
Selection and arrangement copyright © Helen Exley 2004
The moral rights of the authors have been asserted.

12 11 10 9 8 7 6

ISBN 1-86187-426-X

Printed in China.

Exley Publications Ltd, 16 Chalk Hill, Watford, Herts WD19 4BG, UK
Exley Publications LLC, 185 Main Street, Spencer, MA 01562, USA
www.helenexleygiftbooks.com

Utterly adorable cats

HANA DEKA CLUB®

© 2004 YONEO MORITA
Licensed by Intercontinental Ltd

A HELEN EXLEY GIFTBOOK

I purr and your blues fade away.
I snuggle close
and frown turns to smile.
I play chase
and your world fills with laughter.
And in return,
all I ask, is two meals a day...
...and all your love.

SOFTIE, B.2004

From the tip of her ears
to the tip of her tail
a kitten demands,
"Love me please."

MEOW-MEOW, 2004

Got to love me – I'm the kitten!

FAUX PAWS, B.2003

I'm a little confectio

hat will melt your heart.

KIT E. ANGEL, B.2003

All I ask is
that you love me
half as much
as I love myself.

MOLLY MOGG, 2001

The more love a cat receives
the cuter she becomes.

PUMPKIN, 1984

The human has not been born who will not weaken in resolve at the sight of a poor, cute cat in pathetic distress. Begin by sitting outside your chosen victim's house meowing pitifully. You will notice her frequently peeping out at you through the window. Keep meowing and soon she will appear at the door with a saucer of milk. Now use your full acting skills, limp slowly across to the saucer as if in pain and lap up the milk pretending you have had nothing for weeks. If possible rub against her legs – such contact tugs at a human's heartstrings. When the milk is finished sit in your cutest way, purr appreciatively and look straight into her eyes. This will completely break down any remaining resistance. Instantly you will be invited in to take over her heart and home and will be pampered until you decide to move on.

Dogs are dogs,
birds are birds

cats are gods.

ANCIENT CAT SCHOLAR

CHERISH YOUR PAST —

THOSE GOLDEN TIMES

WHEN THE ANCIENT EGYPTIANS

TREATED YOUR ANCESTORS

AS GODS.

YOU TOO MUST EXPECT,

INDEED INSIST UPON,

SIMILAR DEVOTION.

MARIGOLD (1866-1873)

A human should never attempt
to tell a cat what to do.
She may attempt to get us to do something
by begging, bribing, beseeching,
sweet-talking, appealing, imploring,
flattering. Even then we will probably
just ignore her.

MOGG II

Never ask for what you want

– always demand.

TOM CAT

Cats sleep because it is their
sole purpose in life.
Humans sleep so that they
have the energy to serve their cat.

*If at first you don't succeed
it's time to take another nap.*

PUSS ZI, 4,200 B.C.

Sometimes I feel sorry
for my domestic.
I wake him at 2 a.m.
to get out, at 4 a.m.
to get back in again and at 6 a.m.
to make my breakfast.
If he accidentally wakes me
while vacuuming I get quite cross
and sulk for hours.

FLUFFBALL

I own the house —
they just pay the mortgage.

SAM OSCAR

My human thinks that I'm arrogant,
selfish, lazy, and huffy.
She's right and I have many other
fine virtues too.

PUSSYKINS, B.1998

What are little kittens made of?

% cuteness

29 % mischief

28 % purrs

10 % soft fur

3% innocence

*All things come
to those who purr.*

There are many secrets
to getting out of trouble when
you have done something bad.
Look indignant.
Purr sweetly.
Pretend to be injured.
Blame the dog.
Run like Hell.

OLIVER, B.2002

THE PHILOSOPHY OF A CAT

If I leave the room my slave
ceases to exist.
When I return she mysteriously
becomes real once more.
Paradoxically when she leaves the room
I do not cease to exist –
but she does.

I purr therefore I am.

I sleep therefore I am happy.

I meow therefore I am fed.

CATFUCIOUS, 598 B.C.

Dedicated scratching of wallpaper
is the key to all knowledge.

CATTO, 1680

CAT DICTIONARY

Insomnia –
The inability to get more than twenty hours sleep in a day.

Loyalty –
Staying with the one human for more than six weeks.

Stress –
A condition only observed in other creatures.

Bird –
Canned food with wings but no can.

Flea –
A tiny vicious dragon.

Dog –
A large hairy overgrown flea.

Consciousness –
That annoying time between naps.

Food –
Something which must be taken at 30-minute intervals.

Love –
A feeling one can only truly have for oneself.

Box –
A possible portal to utopia which must be
explored and guarded.

Work –
An activity carried out by mankind
to maintain catkind in comfort.

Humility –
No known definition.

MATHEMATICS OF PROBABILITY:

The chance of a cat doing anything its human wants it to do equals zero.

Don't come running when your human calls —
follow this strict protocol:-
Acknowledge that you have heard his pleas
by ignoring him completely.
Continue, slowly, with whatever you are doing.
Take a long, long nap.
Of course — all of the above
should be completely ignored
at the word, "dinner".

FELIX, THE PHILOSOPHER

Make your home wherever
you can find a suitable sucker
to tend to all your needs with love
and devotion.
If fortune blesses, make many homes.

ADAGE OF CAT GODDESS BASTET, c.998 B.C.

A cat can hear a mouse
yawning a mile away
while filtering out the sound
of a pleading human
who is just six feet away.

DAILY KARMA FOR KALMER CATS

00:00 – 07:00 Sleep on bed

07:00 – 07:10 Breakfast

07:10 – 12:00 Morning Respite on cooker

12:00 – 12:10 Lunch

12:10 – 15:00 Peaceful Contemplation

15:00 – 15:01 Exercise (Optional)

15:01 – 18:00 Meditate in a sunny spot

18:00 – 18:15 Dinner

18:15 – 00:00 Evening Reflection in drawer

A wise cat acquires wisdom
through spending
long periods motionlessly
staring into space
considering issues
of universal importance –
such as,
"Where shall I sleep next?".

Every warmed cushion
is made for a cat
Every sunbeam finds a cat.

To sing is human, to meow divine.

HOUSE RULES FOR MY HUMAN

Keep to your own, very small,
part of the bed.
Keep my chair warm while I'm out playing.
Make sure my best-loved "Tom and Jerry"
is always on the television.
Do not get irritated when I put my paw
in your mouth to stop you snoring.
Be attentive to my every need
twenty-four hours a day.
Accept my little presents
of dead mice gratefully.
Reward my kindness by buying salmon regularly.
Never wake me – except for dinner.
Avoid all movement in bed
so as not to disturb me.
Above all accept that there can be only
one boss in the house – Me.

AGATHA, 2004

One cream cake
in the paw
is worth two in
the refrigerator.

Quantum Cat Theory:
Upon hearing the sound of a can
being opened,
it becomes possible for a cat
to travel faster
than the speed of light.

When I'm out
I want to be in.
When I'm in
I want to be out.
And often
I want to be in and out
all at the same time.

*Sometimes
the opposite of
out is out.*

CAT NIGHTMARES

Becoming slave to man.
Furballs.
Having to go "walkies" on a lead.
Mice seeking revenge.
Baths.
Having to be nice to dogs.
Fleas the size of crows.
Being stuck up a tree.
Broken can openers.

Any noise worth making is worth making, at full volume, in the middle of the night.

Should you accidentally find yourself
out in the cold, dark, scary dead of night
don't suffer in silence.
Wail loudly and persistently –
your human will happily get out of bed
to come to your rescue and prepare
you a midnight snack.

SIMBA

A hungry cat scorns her human.

A well fed cat scorns her human too.

CAESAR, 542

All humans are equal, whether you take up residence with a princess in a palace or a poor old lady in a tiny basement they must be treated in exactly the same manner – with considerable disdain.

VINCENT MOGG, B.1998

No matter how busy you are try to take time out to appreciate the arts. Spend a few moments clawing some expensive wallpaper then lie back, relax, and enjoy your creative efforts.

TAPIOCA

Home is where my king size bed is.

FAT BOY FELIX, B. 1997

EXTRACT FROM
THE SUPREME CAT ORACLE

On this date, October 7, 1999,
it has been decreed that no cat will ever answer
to any of the following humiliating names:

Puss, Pussykins, Fluffly, Fluffles, Oink,
Dandy Lion, Kitty, Fluffball, Ding-A-Ling,
Fleabag, Furball, Fur Face, Dog,
Fang, Fat Boy, Faux Paws, Zwingli, Rambo,
Ratbag, Dixie-Belle, What-a-mess,
Kit Kat, Raggedy Ann, Occupant,
Rumblepurr, Meow-Meow....

Chairman Meow

As I look out from my cosy window-ledge
I see thousands of humans working hard
in the blazing sun to construct
huge pyramids.
Yet for all their achievements
they do not seem happy
or content. When will they learn
from us that happiness
is to be found in the simple things –
like a wooden box
and that the real measure of success
is how long you manage to sleep in a day.

SAMANTHA, 2001 B.C.

A life devoid of cream
is a life without purpose.

Nothingness is what exists
when the food bowl is empty.

MOGG (1989-1997)

A SIMPLE REQUEST

Let me in.
Let me out.
Feed me.
Talk to me.
Play with me.
Groom me.
Leave me in peace.
Adore me.
Please!

LA CHATTE, 1844

As I grow old
I will catch fewer mice.
I will play less and less.
I will sleep day and night.
This is the time when
you will need to love me most.

VICTORIA, B.1996

CAT CALISTHENICS

The best time to perform your workout
is 3 a.m. when the house is perfectly quiet
and your human is comfortably asleep in bed.
Warm up with a few stretches –
extending legs fully and retracting them slowly,
pulling your claws across the sofa with
a comforting rasping sound.
Practise the "Hunt Mouse" routine
by chasing a small ball around the room –
be careful to avoid falling vases as you charge
frantically over tables and chairs.
Next, stretch each claw in turn as high
up the wall as you can possibly reach,
leave a mark on the wallpaper
as a target to beat next time.
Finally sprint at top speed into your human's
bedroom, leap onto his tummy, relax
and drift off to sleep.

RAMBO, 2003

NEW YEAR RESOLUTIONS

I promise, on cold wintry nights,
to make the correct decision
on whether or not to wake my human
to let me out or just to poo on the carpet.
I will try my hardest not to sick up a mouse head
while my human is having dinner.
I will try not to ignore my human quite so often.
I resolve not to pretend
I don't like canned food when there's
fresh salmon in the refridgerator.
I promise not to treat my human
condescendingly – too often.
I promise not to cause my human revulsion
by eating spiders.
I resolve not to share my fleas.

KIKKI, 2004

If the laws of evolution hold true
then through time humans
will eventually become
completely perfect — that is,
they will evolve into cats.

PUMPKIN PUSS, B.1997

What I like doing best is Nothing.
I can spend a huge amount of time
doing Nothing without ever tiring of it.
The best time for doing Nothing
is when your humans
are rushing about doing Everything
and you just lie back comfortably, watching.

MISS FLUFFY, 2004

WHEN CATS RULE THE WORLD

Just as today – Humans will be our slaves.

Vets will be banned.

Bowls will always be full.

Dogs will be small and fun to chase.

Mice will come in a variety of tastes.

Tin cans will not have lids.

There will be 40 hours in each day

to allow more time for sleeping.